DISCLAIMER NOTICE:

This ebook illuminates the path towards optimal vitality, flourishing wellness, and enlightened nourishment, and is crafted for edification and inspiration. However, it must be emphasized that these teachings are strictly for educational purposes and are in no way a substitution for or replacement of the wisdom and guidance of a physician or other revered health-care professional. Should you retain any hesitations or queries regarding the flourishing of your being, always seek out the counsel of those who walk the path of holistic healing. Dismissing, sidestepping, or postponing the wise directions of your health-care professional as a result of the gleanings of this ebook is strongly not advised.

Consulting with your physician prior to commencing any exercise program or making significant changes to your diet, such as incorporating supplements, or nutrition plans.

Nothing in this eBook is intended to be, or should be interpreted as, medical or counseling care. For the purposes of this disclosure, the practice of medicine and counseling includes, but is not limited to, psychiatry, psychology, psychotherapy, or providing health care treatment, instructions, diagnosis, prognosis or advice.

PREFACE

Welcome to High Vibe Grubbing, a book dedicated to helping you discover the power of high-vibration foods and their ability to transform your energy levels, health, and overall well-being.

As our lives become more hectic and fast-paced, it's easy to reach for quick, convenient foods that are often low in nutrients and high in processed ingredients. However, this diet can leave us feeling depleted, sluggish, and unfulfilled. On the other hand, high-vibration foods are natural, whole foods packed with nutrients, vitamins, and minerals. These foods provide sustained energy throughout the day, improve digestion, and reduce inflammation, among other health benefits.

This book will explore a range of high-vibration foods and how to incorporate them into your daily meals. I will also share tips and recipes for creating delicious and healthy dishes that will energize and satisfy you. We aim to empower you to take charge of your health and make food choices that support your overall well-being.

PREFACE

Every person deserves to feel vibrant, healthy, and energized, and we hope that this ebook will help you achieve just that.

Thank you for choosing High Vibe Grubbing as your guide to a healthier, more energized you. Let's get started!

INTRODUCTION

Unlock your true potential with High Vibe Grubbing! We delve into the power of consuming high-vibrational foods and their capacity to positively influence our physical and spiritual wellbeing. By providing our bodies with food that is in tune with our highest selves, we can open the door to increased well-being, higher energy levels, and a greater sense of serenity. With the correct balance, we can construct a life of abundance, vitality, and joy. Join us on our mission to unlock your ultimate potential!

To truly understand living a life of high vibrancy, one must understand that it is a life of vitality, positivity, and faith in a greater power. This power is a force of love, wisdom, intelligence, wealth, and peace that is within each of us, and which seeks to express itself through us in order to manifest the desires of our hearts and enjoy all the good things life has to offer. When we recognize the presence of love and life, we are in the realm of God, experiencing this incredible force.

INTRODUCTION CONT'D

This realm of boundless potential lies open to all who will but only believe and reach out to experience the divine Spirit of Life. Encounter this life-giving Spirit which desires to flow through and around you to others. This realm is the realm of creation, which operates on the highest vibrational energy, expressing itself through all things.

The universe is powered by vibrational energy, and energy attracts like energy; spiritual forces will not lower their vibrations to meet you; you must elevate your vibrations to connect with them. The more you abide in higher vibrational energy, you open yourself up to the spiritual realm of God, which is not formed from religious beliefs but from the spirit within the God of your understanding. Prayer, meditation, praise, gratitude, and self-love elevate your vibrational energy. On the other hand, negative emotions such as anger, bitterness, jealousy, disempowering thoughts, and poor health all work to lower your vibration and create adverse reactions.

CONTENTS

CHAPTER
01
Understanding the Power of Vibrational Energy in Creating a Balanced Life

CHAPTER
02
Starting your day with gratitude

CHAPTER
03
My Daily Grub

CHAPTER
04
Vibing -n- Spicing

CHAPTER
05

Vibing, Grubbing, Eating your colors!

CHAPTER
06
The Sun be Vibing

Understanding the Power of Vibrational Energy in Creating a Balanced Life'

01

Vibrational energy

is the kinetic energy produced by the oscillations of atoms, molecules, and particles. This energy is generated through the movement of these particles, and its frequency determines the magnitude of energy produced. Every human being is born with a unique and powerful vibration expressed through the body's motions and sounds. This energy is thought to be linked to one's feelings, ideas, and aspirations. By understanding and channeling this energy, one can become more in tune with their inner self and manifest their intentions. To do this, one must become aware of the energy within and learn its power through prayer, meditation, visualization, and other spiritual practices. Once the energy is understood and mastered, it can produce the desired result.

All creation is connected through the vibrant energy of frequencies and vibrations, an invisible force that can be felt and seen.

01

Our physical bodies

too, are composed of this energy, ever in motion and responsive to our thoughts and emotions. We can use this powerful energy to manifest our desires and create the life of our dreams. By comprehendingresponsive and utilizing this vibrational energy, we gain access to a world of potential and can transform our lives to better the lives of our plans. By learning and using this vibrational energy, we gain access to a world of possibility and can improve our lives. Positive and negative vibrational energies can have a profound and transformative impact on one's emotional life. Positive vibrations can help fill one with a sense of power, optimism, and hope, while negative vibrations can lead to fear, anxiety, and depression. Positive vibrations can help bolster one's self-esteem and confidence, while negative vibrations can lead to self-doubt and insecurity.

01

Such energies

can be seen in many aspects of one's life, from relationships to work to mental health. It is essential to recognize the power of vibrational energies and to take steps to balance them to achieve emotional well-being.

Food plays an integral role in a person's vibrational energy, and nourishing the body with the proper nutrients can help to boost one's energy levels and make one feel more vibrant and alive. Eating a balanced diet, rich in fruits, vegetables, and whole grains, not only provides the body with the necessary vitamins, minerals, and other vital nutrients, but it can also help to ensure that one's energy remains high and their connection to the environment remains strong. On the other hand, consuming processed, sugary, and unhealthy foods can have the opposite effect, often leading to lethargy, fatigue, and low energy levels. Eating well is essential for maintaining high vibrational energy and feeling energized, alive, and connected to the world.

01

It is essential

to maintain a high vibrational frequency, as this enables us to remain connected to our genuine, authentic selves. We can become more receptive to our environment and the Universe through this connection. This can help us to bring our dreams into reality, attract positive energy, and ultimately lead a more meaningful life. Also, keeping high vibrational energy can help us heal from past traumas and cultivate healthier relationships. By connecting to our true selves and allowing our power to move freely, we can experience more joy and live more abundantly.

01

Vibrational energy

is the life force that animates us all, and it is something that every person has the potential to cultivate. People are born with a specific vibrational frequency, but it can be heightened or diminished depending on their environment. For example, positive thoughts, prayer, meditation, and other mindful practices can access high vibrational energies. To raise one's vibrational frequency, engaging in activities that bring joy and peace into one's life is essential. This could include spending time in nature, nourishing the body with healthy foods, and engaging in spiritual practices that bring a sense of connection and oneness. Additionally, one should avoid engaging in activities that may result in negative emotions, such as gossiping, watching negative news, or engaging in unhealthy behaviors. Doing so allows one to tap into their highest vibrational frequency and experience abundant joy and peace.

01

When a person

is vibrating at a higher frequency, they can experience inner peace and connection. This can lead to greater mental clarity, improved physical health, and a greater likelihood of attracting favorable circumstances into their life. On the contrary, lower vibrations can manifest as feelings of anxiety, fear, unhappiness, and physical ailments such as headaches, fatigue, and digestive troubles. In addition, lower vibrations can be caused by negative thoughts and behaviors, an unhealthy diet, and too much time spent in front of screens. Therefore, to reduce the lower vibrations, focusing on positive thinking and activities and spending time outdoors in nature is essential.

02

Starting your day with gratitude

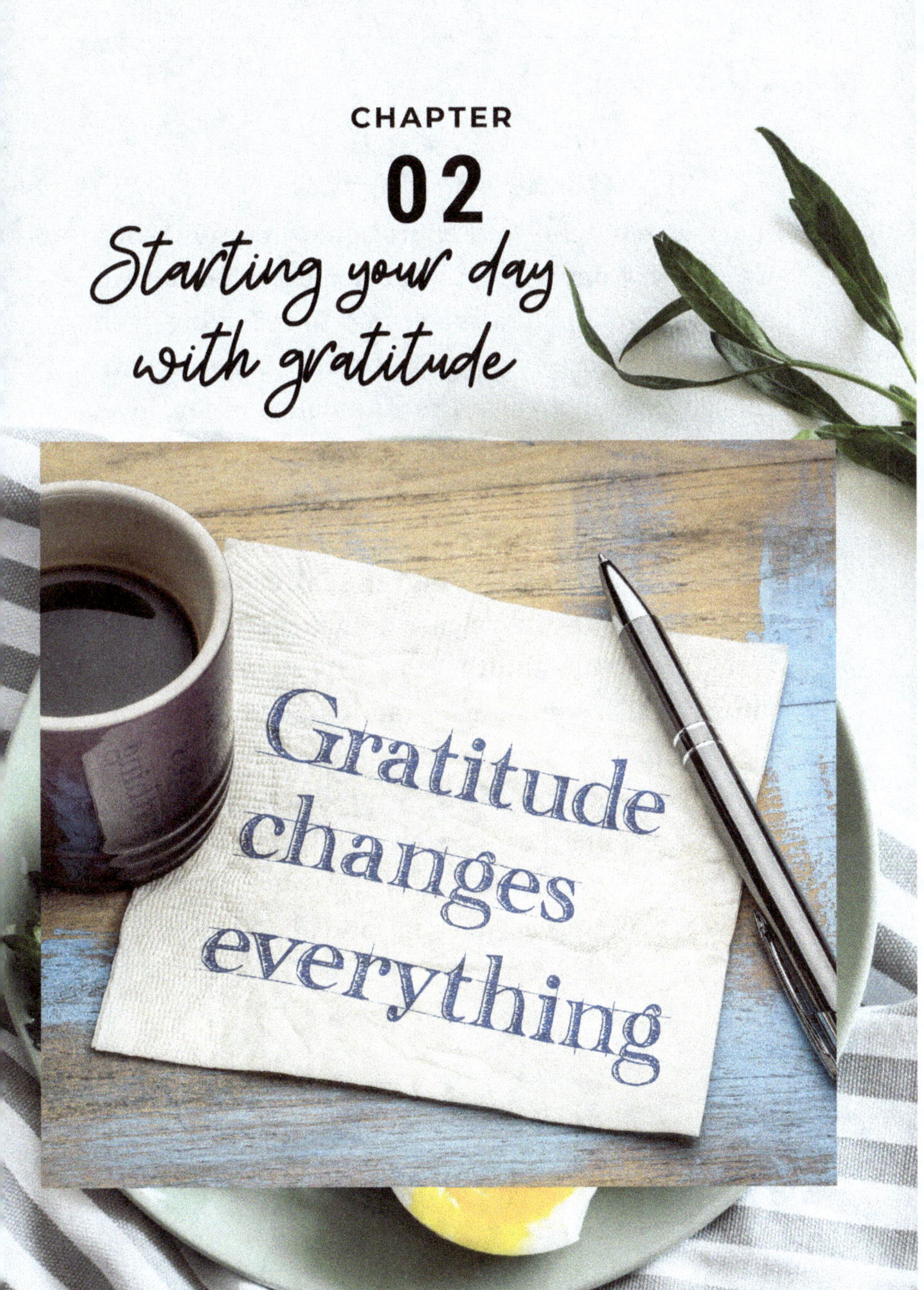

Gratitude is a vital

part of elevating our vibrational energy. When we express our appreciation for the blessings in our lives, we open ourselves up to receiving even more of these gifts. Gratitude helps us to recognize and cherish the abundance of joy, love, and peace that already exists in our lives. By expressing gratitude for what we have, we are more likely to focus on the positive aspects of our lives. Acknowledging the already present good allows us to release any negative energy blocking our ability to experience higher vibrational frequencies. Practicing gratitude can also help us to connect more deeply with ourselves and the world around us, fostering a greater sense of peace and contentment. Cultivating gratitude can raise our vibrational energy, bringing us more joy and abundance.

Gratefulness

can open us up to new opportunities, relationships, and experiences that can help us to raise our vibrational energy even further. Incorporating gratitude into our lives daily can be a potent tool for increasing our vibrational energy and living a life of joy and abundance. Gratitude can also help us to cultivate deeper connections with others. When we practice gratitude, we can recognize the gifts that others bring to our lives and express our appreciation for them. This helps to build trust and understanding between people, as well as foster a profound connection. Gratitude can also allow us to become more mindful and present in our lives. By taking the time to savor the present moment and be thankful for what we have, we can become more aware of our surroundings and be more in tune with our inner selves. This can help us better manage stress and anxiety and make the most of our days.

02

Practicing gratitude

can also help us to connect more deeply with ourselves and the world around us, fostering a more profound sense of peace and contentment. Ultimately, cultivating a sense of gratitude can help raise our vibrational energy, bringing us more joy and abundance. Gratefulness can open us up to new opportunities, relationships, and experiences that can help us to raise our vibrational energy even further. Practicing gratitude regularly can be a potent tool for growing our vibrational energy and living a life of joy and abundance. Finally, gratitude can open the door to a life of purpose and profound significance. By recognizing the beauty in our lives and expressing our heartfelt gratitude for it, we can begin to craft a meaningful and enriching life. We can focus on the moments that bring us joy and make us feel truly alive. This can help us discover our true calling and live a rewarding and fulfilling life.

My Daily Grub

03

Food

can undeniably affect our energetic vibration. Incorporating fresh, nutrient-rich, plant-based foods into our diet can provide us with the energy we need to sustain and elevate our vibrations. Food can be a powerful agent for raising our vibrational energy. Eating foods packed with antioxidants, minerals, and vitamins can assist us in feeling more energized and lift our vibration. These foods include fresh fruits and vegetables, nuts and seeds, and omega-3 fatty acids in fish and other seafood. Furthermore, foods high in protein can help boost our energy levels, whereas foods high in sugar can actually lower our vibration. Therefore, it is essential to be mindful of the types of food we consume and focus on eating foods promoting a higher vibration.

Different colors

of food can profoundly affect a person's vibrational energy, influencing emotions, moods, and even physical health. For example, consuming red or orange foods can invigorate the body and stimulate energy levels, while blue or purple foods have a calming, relaxing effect. Dark leafy greens, like kale and spinach, contain magnesium and iron, which can help to boost energy levels and harmonize the body's energy. Additionally, yellow and white foods can help to increase mental clarity and focus. Thus, it is important to be mindful of the colors of food we consume, and to include a variety of colors in our diets to maximize our vibrational energy.

Keeping

our vibrational frequency high is important because it affects our overall wellbeing. When we are in a high vibration, we are more likely to experience joy, peace, and positive energy. This can also benefit our physical health, allowing us to stay healthier and stronger. Additionally, when we are in a high vibrational state, we can better manifest our desires and goals. Therefore, keeping our vibrational frequency high is important to experience the best of life. Vibrational foods remain close to their natural state, imbued with the energetic vibrations of the Earth and the Sun. These foods carry the power to nourish us on multiple levels, both physically and spiritually, and they can be a gateway to a deeper connection with the natural world.

Breakfast Grub

Starting the day with a high vibrational breakfast is an ideal way to energize and nourish your body. Such a meal offers a balanced combination of vitamins, minerals, and antioxidants, which can help reduce inflammation and support your immune system. Examples of a high vibrational breakfast include oatmeal with fresh fruit and nuts, a smoothie made with almond milk, banana, spinach, and chia seeds, or a bowl with quinoa, vegetables, and a poached egg. Eating a nutrient-dense breakfast helps to keep your blood sugar levels stable and gives your body sustained energy throughout the day. Ultimately, a high vibrational breakfast provides you with the nourishment and vitality you need to start your day off with a bang and keep you energized and healthy all day.

Breakfast Grub

Eggs are considered a high-vibrational food because they are a complete protein, containing all nine essential amino acids. The egg yolk is also rich in vitamins and minerals, including B vitamins, Vitamin A, Selenium, Iron, and Zinc. In addition, when appropriately cooked, eggs are a great source of healthy fats, providing essential fatty acids such as omega-3s. Omelets are another high-vibrational energy breakfast option. Fill your omelet with your favorite vegetables and top it with a sprinkle of cheese for an even more flavorful breakfast. If you're in a rush, try scrambling some eggs with some diced vegetables and topping it with a dollop of salsa for a quick and easy breakfast that will leave you feeling energized and ready for the day ahead.

Nourish your body

and soul with vibrant smoothies made with fresh, organic ingredients. First, fill your cup with nutrient-dense fruits, vegetables, nuts, and seeds, and infuse it with superfoods like spirulina, chia, bee pollen, and more. Then, select plant-based proteins such as hemp, flax, and chia to boost essential vitamins and minerals. Not only will these smoothies make you feel good, but they will also tantalize your taste buds!

03

Smoothie #1 Refreshed

INGREDIENTS

- 1 cup of chopped apples,
- 1 cup of chopped mangos,
- 1 cup of chopped strawberries,
- 1 heaping hand of chopped kale,
- 1 tablespoon of ground flaxseed,
- 2 tablespoon of freshly grated ginger
- 12 oz organic coconut water

This high vibration smoothie rich in fiber brings together the sweet, tart and healthful flavors of apples, mangos, strawberries, kale and fresh ginger with the creamy, cooling and hydrating properties of coconut water.

03

Smoothie #2
Green Banana

INGREDIENTS

- 1 cup frozen blueberries,
- 1 cup unsweetened almond milk, (adjust according to your preference)
- 1 ripe banana,
- 1 hand full spinach,
- dash cinnamon
- 1 table ground flaxseed for added nutrition and fiber.

Here is a high-vibrational smoothie recipe that you can use to create a nourishing and delicious drink. This smoothie is a great way to start your day, or you can enjoy it as a healthy snack option anytime. It is packed with nutrients and antioxidants, and the ground flaxseed provides a good source of fiber. Enjoy this smoothie for a boost of energy and vitality!

03

Lunch Grub

Eating a high-vibration lunch is essential for sustaining positive, vibrant energy throughout the day. Such a meal should be composed of fresh, organic, and nutrient-dense ingredients that are unprocessed, such as fresh fruits, nuts and seeds, whole grains, and healthy proteins like lean meats, fish, eggs, and legumes, homemade soups, smoothies and juices, full grain wraps, and steamed vegetables. You can also add healthy fats like nuts, avocados, and olive oil.

Lunch Grub

A balanced lunch, full of vitamins and minerals, will help to keep you energized and focused throughout the day.

A high vibrational lunch can begin most delightfully with a vibrant, fresh fruit salad, which is not only a delectable and nourishing start to the meal, but also helps to usher in a powerful and positive energy to the table. To add more nutrition, sprinkle nuts or seeds and drizzle a Raspberry vinaigrette over a bed of leafy greens. A flavorful veggie stir fry with some grains like quinoa or wild rice would be the ideal accompaniment for the main dish. Finally, a piece of dark, rich chocolate would be the perfect treat to finish the meal. This meal will surely bring a bright, high vibrational energy to the day.

03

Dinner Grub

Eating a high-vibrational dinner is essential to cultivating a healthy lifestyle. A high-vibrational dinner should contain fresh, organic, unprocessed, and nutrient-dense ingredients. The more wholesome the components, the more elevated the vibrational energy of the meal. Eating a high-vibrational dinner can help to improve overall well-being, increase vitality, and enhance mental clarity. Moreover, a high-vibe dinner may help to reduce stress levels and promote a sense of relaxation. Eating a highly nutritional meal can benefit both physical and emotional health. These dinners are not only savory and nutritious meals but also elevate your energy levels. Some examples include salads made with fresh vegetables, zucchini noodles with pesto, and quinoa bowls with roasted vegetables.

03

Dinner Grub

Other beneficial high-vibe dinners are stir-fries with vegetables and lean proteins, tacos with plant-based proteins and vegetables, and vegan soups. By integrating fresh and nutritious ingredients into your meals, you can ensure that your dinners are both delectable and high in vibration.

Create a dinner that will bring your mind, body, and spirit into a high-vibration state. Start with a salad made with organic, locally sourced ingredients. Then enjoy wild-caught seafood, sweet potatoes, and locally grown vegetables. Finish the meal with dark chocolate or a tart made with seasonal fruit.

03

Vibing Grilled Salmon

INGREDIENTS

- 1 lb wild caught salmon
- 1/4 cup lemon herb butter
- 2 cups sweet potatoes dice cubes
- 1/4 cup sliced almonds (optional)
- 1 bag fresh spinach
- 1/4 cup cherry tomatoes sliced
- 1/4 cup sliced green onions
- 1/4 cup chopped fresh parsley
- 1 Table min iced garlic
- 2 Table extra virgin olive oil
- Salt & pepper to taste

Vibing Spice Glaze

- 2 tea lemon juice
- 1/2 cup white wine
- 2 table balsamic vinegar
- 1/2 cup Raw honey
- 2 tea dijon mustard
- 1/2 tea garlic powder
- ½ tea onion powder
- 1/2 tea black pepper
- 1/2 tea chili powder

Instructions

1. Preheat oven to 400 degrees. A great option is an air fryer.

2. Place sweet potatoes cubes in bowl, drizzle with 1 Tablespoon of olive oil and sprinkle with cinnamon and cardamon toss until evenly covered, place on a baking sheet. Bake for 15-20 minutes, or until tender.

3. In a small saute pan, heat 1 Tablespoon Olive oil over medium heat. Stir in spinach, tomatoes, green onions, and parsley. Set aside

4. Brush salmon with herb butter set aside

Vibing Spice Glaze

Instructions Cont'd

5. In a small sauce pan, whisk together lemon juice, wine, vinegar, honey, mustard, garlic powder, onion powder, black pepper, salt, and chili powder. Cook over medium heat allowing slow boil until lightly thicken set aside from heat.

6. Brush salmon with *Vibing Spice Glaze*, bake for about 10 minutes, or until salmon is cooked through. Sprinkle with a little salt and pepper to taste a hint of lemon. Plate and serve!

Viben Chocolate Desert

Delight your taste buds with this delectable high vibrational dark chocolate dessert! This dessert is both nutritious and indulgent. The dark chocolate and coconut flakes provide a boost of antioxidants that will leave you feeling energized and satisfied. Enjoy this healthy and delicious treat today!

- 2 cups of dark chocolate chips
- 1/3 cup of honey,
- 1 teaspoon of cinnamon,
- 1/4 cup of cocao powder,
- 1/4 cup of coconut flakes, and a dash of sea salt.

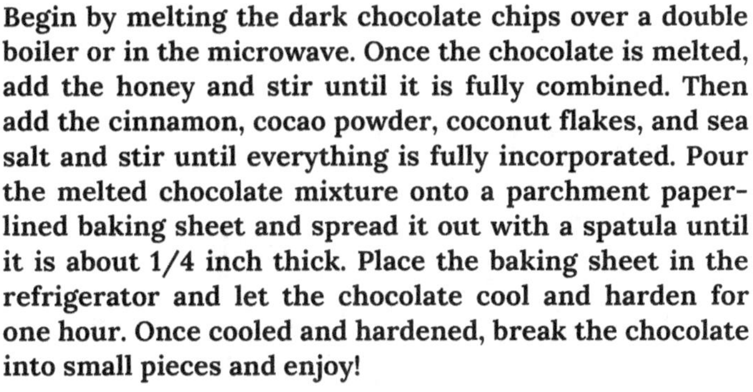

Begin by melting the dark chocolate chips over a double boiler or in the microwave. Once the chocolate is melted, add the honey and stir until it is fully combined. Then add the cinnamon, cocoa powder, coconut flakes, and sea salt and stir until everything is fully incorporated. Pour the melted chocolate mixture onto a parchment paper-lined baking sheet and spread it out with a spatula until it is about 1/4 inch thick. Place the baking sheet in the refrigerator and let the chocolate cool and harden for one hour. Once cooled and hardened, break the chocolate into small pieces and enjoy!

03

Cooking for the soul

Soul food is a cuisine deeply rooted in African American culture, emphasizing family, love, and togetherness. On a Sunday afternoon or a Friday night fish fry, a mother or grandmother would display their love, passion, and culinary talent in the kitchen, crafting dishes like black-eyed peas, okra, sweet potatoes, mac & cheese, and collard greens. Mommas would spend hours shucking, cooking, and baking with fresh ingredients, creating meals from the love in their soul. This cuisine, made with the highest vibration of love, brought family and friends together uniquely and specially.

Today

Today we too can create high-vibe grub with that same love, using fresh, locally sourced ingredients and cooking with herbs and spices to bring out unique flavors. Use organic fruits and vegetables, whole grains, nuts, and seeds to make high-vibe grub for the soul. These ingredients can be cooked in various ways, such as steaming, sautéing, or grilling. The dishes can also be seasoned with herbs and spices like garlic, cumin, and turmeric to help bring out the flavors. Combining these ingredients can create a delicious meal packed with flavor and nutrients while also providing vital minerals and an added layer of flavor.

03

When preparing

soul food, high-vibe ingredients are simmered over low heat, allowing the flavors to marry together and create a richer flavor. This method of cooking, known as "simmering," helps to retain the nutrients and minerals in the food and bring out the flavor. Cooking for the soul begins in the heart, and using high-vibe ingredients and soulful cooking methods, we can create meals that nourish our bodies and spirits.

03

Remember

Remember that food is life-giving energy and that the enthusiasm and passion you put into your cooking will create an atmosphere of joy and pleasure that your family will surely appreciate. So enjoy preparing home-cooked meals and savor the satisfaction of nourishing and loving your loved ones.

Vibing -n- Spicing

04

Spices

have long been used as an alchemical tool to enhance flavor, add complexity to dishes, and provide curative benefits. In addition, these high-vibration spices can nurture the body and spirit from cinnamon to cumin. Here is a list of some of the most potent spices and how to best use them to support your body's wellbeing. From warming cinnamon to energizing cumin, these spices can stimulate the senses, invigorate the body, and promote spiritual well-being.

Just a few Spices

Basil- a powerhouse of antioxidants, helps to combat free radicals, benefits digestion and is excellent for the skin. It is used in teas, soups, and sauces to add flavor and various health benefits. By adding these high-vibrational spices to your daily routine, you can reap the healing benefits and add some extra flavor to your meals!

Black pepper - is rich in antioxidants and can help boost immunity when added to curries and other savory dishes.

Cardamom - is a warming spice that can aid digestion when added to teas, yogurts, and desserts.

Cayenne Pepper can reduce inflammation and improve circulation, adding a pinch of heat to any dish. In addition, these spices can add flavor, nutrition, and vibrancy to any meal.

Cinnamon: This spice is a potent anti-inflammatory and helps to boost circulation, as well as reduce fatigue and improve digestion. Add it to your morning coffee or tea, or sprinkle it over your favorite breakfast cereal.

Just a few Spices

Cloves - containing the antioxidant and anti-inflammatory eugenol, can be used to enhance both savory dishes and sweet desserts.

Cumin - This earthy spice has been used for centuries to help aid digestion and boost immunity. Try adding it to rice dishes, tacos, or use it to make a flavorful hummus.

Ginger - This spicy root is known for its anti-nausea properties, and can also help to reduce muscle pain and improve circulation. Ginger can be added to teas and smoothies, or used to make a spicy stir-fry.

Oregano - contains a number of chemicals that may help reduce coughs and aid digestion, while also providing protection against certain bacteria and viruses. Its uses in soups, sauces, and teas..

Sage - a veritable powerhouse of antioxidants, not only supports oral health and helps alleviate symptoms of menopause, but can also be used in teas, stuffings when roasting, and added to a variety of tomato dishes.

Turmeric - This bright yellow spice is a powerful anti-inflammatory and has been shown to help reduce joint pain. Try adding it to curries, soups, and stews, or use it to make a delicious golden milk.

04

High Vibe Tea

Countless studies have shown that teas can boost your immune system and help improve your overall health. Green and white teas are potent anti-oxidants that support excellent health, such as Chamomile, Lavender, Rose Tea, Ginger,Peppermint, and Matcha Green Tea. Although there are countless teas to try, ensure high quality teas are purchased.

Vibing, Grubbing, Eating your colors!

Colors

In many belief systems and spiritual practices, it is believed that humans possess an ethereal aura, an energy field that radiates from their very being. This aura is thought to be composed of a spectrum of colors, each one representing a different aspect of the individual's emotional and spiritual state.

THE COLOR GREEN

The color green, for instance, is associated with qualities such as compassion, healing, harmony, connection to nature, growth, and renewal. Thus, the presence of a green aura may indicate that an individual is in a state of healing, harmony, and growth.

GREEN LEAFY VEGGIES

Green leafy vegetables can have a profound impact on the human body's energy levels in a variety of ways. For instance, they are nutrient-dense, containing abundant vitamins and minerals essential for energy production. B vitamins, in particular, are abundant and help convert food into energy while supporting healthy brain function.

Greens

Moreover, green leafy vegetables are full of antioxidants that help to reduce oxidative stress and fatigue. In contrast, their high fiber content helps to regulate blood sugar levels and provide sustained energy throughout the day. Chlorophyll, the plant pigment found in abundance in green leafy vegetables, is a powerful fatigue fighter, helping support the body's natural detoxification processes.

Last but not least, green leafy vegetables are high in water content, aiding the body's hydration and preventing fatigue and low energy levels. Incorporating green leafy vegetables into your diet can have a positive impact on energy levels, helping to sustain energy throughout the day and reduce fatigue.

The color Red

Some may interpret the color red in the aura differently or may not believe in the concept of the aura at all. However, the color red is often associated with survival, grounding, security, confidence, passion, and energy. Incorporating the color red into one's diet or environment can help balance and promote feelings of stability and security. Try incorporating foods like beets, red peppers, and tomatoes for added nutritional benefits.

BERRIES

Berries can impact our energy levels in a few different ways. Here are some ways eating berries may help boost our energy. Berries are a good source of carbohydrates, the body's primary fuel source. Berries are packed with vitamins and minerals that the body needs to produce energy. Many berries have a low glycemic index, which means they are digested slowly and release glucose into the bloodstream gradually. This can help provide a steady energy source throughout the day without the sudden spikes and crashes from consuming high-glycemic foods. Incorporating nutrient-rich berries into your diet can be a beneficial way to support your energy levels and bolster your overall health and well-being.

Yellow & Orange Fruits & Veggies

05

In many traditional healing systems, such as Ayurvedic medicine and Traditional Chinese Medicine, it is believed that different foods and colors can profoundly affect the human body's energy. In these systems, yellow and orange are believed to be particularly powerful, promoting personal power, confidence, and self-esteem. This is thought to be due to the color and vibrational energy of these foods and the nutrients they contain. Consuming these foods is supposed to help stimulate the digestive system and promote the transformation of food into energy, which can increase overall vitality and energy levels.

Incorporating yellow and orange fruits and vegetables into one's diet can have various health benefits, including improved immune function, eye health, skin health, and digestive health. Yellow and orange fruits and vegetables are rich in nutrients such as vitamin C, beta-carotene, and other antioxidants, which have a variety of health benefits.

05 Eating a variety of colorful foods

is essential for our bodies to function correctly, as each hue often signifies the presence of different vitamins, minerals, and antioxidants. Colors have long been imbued with spiritual and symbolic meaning, from the shades of the rainbow to the vibrant petals of flowers, the sky, and the plants in nature. The next time you visit the grocery store or farmers market, take a moment to appreciate the natural beauty and harmony of the exuberant produce they offer. Imagine giving your body this amazing life daily. Your taste buds will rejoice at the variety of flavors and energy it encounters with every new bite. It is essential to take time with every meal to give thanks, savor the meal, and enjoy it. The book of Genesis reads, "And God said, Behold, I have given you every herb bearing seed, which is upon the face of all the earth, and every tree, in the which is the fruit of a tree yielding seed; to you, it shall be for meat." Let us be mindful of the earth's bounty and give thanks for providing and preparing our meals.

05 Eating a variety of colorful foods

From a nutritious standpoint, the plants and fruits mentioned in this passage are abundant sources of vitamins, minerals, and other nourishing elements critical for human well-being. In addition, consuming a diet rich in plant-based edibles can have numerous natural and spiritual advantages that bring balance to our souls.

I am not promoting any food diet; I am simply affirming that food is energy. Eating to live is a way of life that honors the body, mind, and soul. It is an intentional act of self-care that nourishes us from the inside out and encourages us to be mindful of the nourishment we provide ourselves. Eating to live is about connecting with the food we consume, understanding its origin and impact on our health, and savoring the flavors and textures of our food. It is about living with intention and purpose and embracing the power of food to fuel our lives.

The Sun be Vibing

06

Every new day

is a precious gift, a chance to create new memories, embark on fresh adventures, and learn and experience the world anew. How you greet the day will set the tone for hours ahead; rising early to bask in the sun's warm embrace, and sipping a cup of High Vibe Tea, is sure to awaken gratitude. The sun is a remarkable blessing, radiating light, heat, and energy, the very lifeblood of our planet. Plants, animals, and humans need the sun; without its heat, the earth would be frozen. Sunlight is essential for human health, providing natural Vitamin D and regulating our circadian rhythm, helping to increase and decrease our melatonin levels. The sun's rays are mighty, helping to fight depression and stress and strengthen our immune system. So, rising early and starting your day with the sun's brilliant embrace has many benefits; it's like the universe greeting the dawn of a new day.

As the Sun Sets

Discovering that particular place, or sitting on your terrace and reveling in the sun's setting, has tremendous benefits for life. After hours spent at the desk on the computer, taking the time to savor the scene of the sun releases stress and tension, restoring relationships and elevating inspirational thought. Watching the beauty of the sun gracefully bowing down for the day, one cannot help but feel grateful for the magnificence and wonders of this universe. Taking a few moments each day to rest, enjoy nature, and lead a balanced life are critical to living a high-vibrational life. Rest allows us to recharge and replenish our energy, and our bodies and minds must function optimally. Nature allows us to reconnect with the natural elements, restoring our equilibrium and reminding us of our place in the larger universe. Balancing our lives with both work and play is also essential in living a high vibrational energy, as it allows us to remain focused and productive while also allowing us to enjoy life and have fun. With this balance, we can maintain a positive outlook and increase our overall energy and vibrational frequency.

As the Sun Sets

As the sun begins to set, preparing for a restful night is essential. Incorporating high-vibrational teas into your daily routine is a great way to relax and unwind. Chamomile, lavender, and peppermint teas are all known to reduce stress, improve sleep quality, and promote feelings of tranquility. Incorporate these teas into your evening ritual for the most restful night possible. This is your life, and how you choose to live, it is entirely up to you. Embracing your daily life with love is the highest vibration that you can achieve.

High Vibe Grubbing is one of the powerful tools you can use to manifest your dreams and desires in this life journey. So here's to a life filled with delicious and nutritious meals!

www.ingramcontent.com/pod-product-compliance
Lightning Source LLC
Chambersburg PA
CBHW050618160726
48003CB00003B/1234